THE
SATANIC
CONSPIRACY

A SPECTER HAUNTING MANKIND

CHARLES MOSCOWITZ

TABLE OF CONTENTS

FORWARD

The thesis of this book, The Satanic Conspiracy, is that a permanent satanic conspiracy has existed and continues to exist within our society, one by which a cabal of elites work both together and separately, formally and informally toward subverting that which is true and good. I present a philosophical and religious case that there is an adversary to God and nature that, when embraced by individuals and groups, seeks to subvert creation, natural law, society and reason.

In my book *God is God* I argue that God is one, that God is good, that God is love, that God is real, and that God is the singular supernatural source of reason and truth. I surmise that God is the creator of the universe and, as such, that God is the creator of all things that are true and that are real, both in the corporal and in the abstract sense. Thus, God, is the creator of all things and is the giver of the laws of nature including the natural laws of man. Yet, in this book about what I contend is a satanic conspiracy, I intend to raise age-old questions such as if God is the creator and if God is love than why is there evil in the world? If God is the creator and if there is no other God than God than did therefore God create evil or is evil an adversary to God? If evil is an adversary to God than would this not contradict the idea of the oneness of the loving God? I will raise such questions as to why, it seems, evil is, at least by appearance, so often rewarded.

I will attempt to tackle paradoxical questions such as how Satan, the evil inclination, and how manifestations of Satan exist in a world that was created by a loving God. I will sketch a brief chronology of individuals and groups that wittingly or unwittingly embraced a satanic conspiracy to subvert God and, as such, to subvert the good. I will attempt to illustrate the un-naturalness of satanic evil and sketch its chronology from antiquity to modern times while analyzing and evaluating the satanic influence today and its complex manifestations.

I will attempt to prove that Satan, or whatever name we might affix to the embodiment of evil, is enthroned when imperfect human beings and societies allow evil to hold sway and that Satan is a force, when not challenged, that threatens the social order as well as the personal life of the individual. I will contrast the satanic influence with that of the good while illustrating the consequences to individuals and to society of the embrace of both the good, Almighty God, and the consequences of the countervailing embrace of Satan.

WHO IS GOD?

In my book *God is God* I argue that God is real and, as such, that an understanding of the existence of God is rational. This principle was well expressed in the American Declaration of Independence:

We hold these truths to be self-evident, that all men are created equal, that they are endowed by their Creator with certain unalienable Rights, that among these are Life, Liberty and the pursuit of Happiness.

In that seminal document, Thomas Jefferson referred to certain *truths*, and to a God who created those certain truths, or those *certain unalienable Rights,* which he described as *self-evident.* Jefferson asserted that those *self-evident* rights emanate from God, the *Creator,* and he identified the creator as the supernatural author of the natural world, as the author of creation. Jefferson, as such, identified the *Creator* as having been separated from the natural world that the *Creator* created.

By referencing *the laws of nature and of nature's God,* Jefferson described unalienable rights as abstract elements of the natural world created by *nature's God.* Jefferson viewed God as the author of such rights, such principles and, more broadly, as the author of all of existence and reality. Jefferson identified rights as not simply invented on the whim of fallible human beings usurping power based upon trickery and artifice, as this would represent the dark aspirations of human nature, but, rather, that rights are in accord with that which is true and, as such, that rights emanate from an infallible source. Indeed, this understanding of rights was the animating principle behind the American claim to independence from the British King who American patriots viewed as the manufacturer of artificial laws created arbitrarily on the whim of a tyrant utilizing fiat power. Americans recognized that the individual was *endowed by the creator,* with unalienable rights that were not, as such, created by or granted by the man-made state or by a cabal of oligarchs.

Thomas Jefferson and much of the American founding generation, in a manner similar to that of other generations in history, struggled to understand the nature of those rights, or natural laws, as well as to understand the nature of laws that were un-natural and, as such, that were man-made. Such laws were perceived as edicts emanating from the tyranny of the British Monarch. The American founding generation struggled with their own conscience the immoral, barbarous and un-natural institution of slavery. They began to ask questions as to whether slavery was natural and moral and, as such, weather it was lawful for one person to own another person like they would own a cord of wood. Jefferson, who was hypocritical on the issue of slavery, nevertheless assumed that natural laws were based upon truths that, while immutable and while outside of human manipulation, were knowable, discoverable, accessible and, to varying degrees, achievable to individuals and society. In the first draft of the Declaration of Independence, Jefferson included explicit language that would have abolished slavery, language that would be cut from the final draft for political reasons. John Adams advanced this foundational principle of American political philosophy when he wrote that *ours is a government of laws and not of men.*

If God is real, if God is good, and if God is the creator of the natural world than the fundamental purpose of human life, given that we possesses degrees of consciousness and free will, is to strive to identify that which is real and that which is good as well as that which is evil and that which is false. Indeed, history is a chronicle of the ongoing human effort to learn, through trial and error, what is true and what is good. Yet human beings are not gods and, as such, we are imperfect beings. We are limited, we are frail, and we view reality and truth through a clouded lens. As imperfect beings, with imperfect perception, we fall into error and, in the active sense, we might from time to time deliberately and to degrees unconsciously choose the path of falsehood and evil. Yet, as beings who possess consciousness and free will we learn from history, individually and collectively, what is true and what is good and we are capable of changing and molding our own lives and of building our futures, as individuals and as nations, with such accumulated knowledge of truth and falsehood serving as our secure foundation.

In the broad sense the philosophical recognition that God is God constitutes a metaphysical understanding that reality is real and that reality and, by extension, that epistemological truths are real and are therefore not merely ideas that are made up whole cloth or manufactured by people. The existence of objective and definable material things, as created by nature's God to use Jefferson's phraseology, offers a blueprint by which we gage and define the nature of existence. This identification is enhanced by our ability to discover and to assimilate abstract truths and morals by means of the accumulated knowledge of what is real and what is true through reason, education, intellect and perception as well as by our innate ability as individuals to know what is moral, to exercise restraint, to engage in logic and to form judgements.   Conversely, the key to overall human and societal progress is likewise based upon the innate ability of individuals, and more broadly, the accumulation of collective wisdom to identify and to know that which is natural and true as well as that which is un-natural, that which is immoral and, as such, that which is false.

I would suggest that one means by which we may prove that God exists is by thinking about the most basic principle of mathematics which is that $0 + 0 = 0$ and that $0 - 0 = 0$. This formula, which is the basis upon which all mathematical theory and formulas are built, proves that something cannot come out of nothing and that, as such, something can only equal something and nothing can only equal nothing. Something can, however, be destroyed and turned into nothing as $1 - 1 = 0$, so, while something can be reduced into nothing, nothing cannot become something. Deriving from this axiom is the assumption that there must have been a starting point for the creation of the universe, which is something, out of the void, which is nothing, assuming that the universe and that all of existence has not simply existed perpetually.

We call that starting point God.

Elements of ancient Greek philosophy, along with modern New Age occultic interpretation of ancient and gnostic texts as well as a simplified view of elements of eastern belief systems view the universe as something that has existed perpetually, as something that has no beginning and that will, as such, have no end. This concept tends toward the view that all living beings are de-facto equal and that all of life exists in an imposed state of perpetual and changeless cycles of generation and regeneration. This theory tends toward the opinion that nothing really changes, that there can ultimately be no real progress or regress and that there is no judgement or ultimate consequence to ideas or to actions. This idea tends to view free-will as a concept that is replaced by pre-ordination with a tendency toward an embrace of the pantheistic belief that God is inside of and is a part of everything that exists. This theory is disproven, I would argue, by a simple observation of such phenomena as erosion in nature, by the laws of physics and mechanics and by the principle of cause and effect in human affairs.

The principle that something was created out of nothing is based upon the biblical creation narrative which mirrors the narratives of most historic civilizations with each holding their own unique permutations and elements within in their understanding of creation. The principle of creation also serves as the basic scientific theorem of western civilization. Indeed, the principle of creation is observable in human society and in individual life as we create things through invention and we change things by harnessing their resources and molding them into something new with our knowledge, our intellect, our hands and our machines. This was how inventors created things like the wheel, refrigeration, the combustible engine, the airplane and the internet as well as works of music, art and architecture. We create material wealth and a standard of living as a result of our creativity and our imagination, our brainpower and our labor, and we develop professional contacts and personal relationships by our choices and by our actions.

17th Century philosopher Rene Descartes, who is most famous for the Latin statement *cogito ergo sum*, which translates as *I think therefore, I am*, proposed that existence is an axiom that is proven by the ability of the individual to perceive a thing outside of himself. This idea, which would animate later enlightenment thinking, mirrors the creation of the universe by a God who created separate essences and entities out of his mind and who created the means by which free-will man possesses the ability to name, by means of language, the separate and distinct identities and aspects of things. In his seminal work *Meditations on First Philosophy*, Descartes, who was a devout Catholic, offered as proof of existence an example of the separate existence of wax. He wrote: *For if I judge that the wax exists because I see it, it would certainly follow more clearly, from the fact that I see it, that I myself exist.* (1.)

While Descartes likely intended to describe the wholistic nature of both the one supernatural God and the individual human being, with each human being holding different attributes within the oneness of the individual life that is capable of identifying various and separate aspects of creation, his ideas nevertheless contributed toward a trend by later enlightenment philosophers and thinkers, including Adam Smith and Karl Marx, who emphasized the dualistic nature of things in and of itself. The trajectory of their particular analysis of Descartes, an analysis that may have been unintended by Descartes who is viewed as one of the founders of modern philosophy and enlightenment thinking, would contribute toward a bifurcation and a modern shattering of the understanding of the oneness of God as the sole source of all of existence and reality, of a God who created all of the various particular aspects of the universe and of life.

When we create and develop physical and abstract things, we imitate, in our own natural and limited context, the supernatural God who created everything out of nothing. While we employ our natural abilities to learn, while we interpret the natural world in order to create the things that either advance or regress our lives and civilization, only God, the creator of the universe creates something out of nothing as the creation of the universe out of nothing would be impossible and, as such, would violate the observable laws of physics and mechanics as well as the abstract laws of mathematics. This is why only a supernatural God could have caused the so-called Big Bang, and yet, something would have had to have happened out of nothing for the Big Bang to have banged not to mention that the so-called Big Bang raises questions regarding how such a bang could have possibly, could have scientifically, if you will, spun off into this complex universe with all of its trillions of moving parts and with all of its designated, interlocking and perfectly designed features and functions. What, or who, caused the Big Bang?

I will tell you who! ... Only Almighty God!

Only God, only the King of the Universe, only the supreme supernatural force existing outside of the created natural universe could have created, with all of its diversity of interlocking elements working in harmony, only the one Almighty God could have caused such a miracle as the universe, the earth, of life itself. Reason indicates that existence could not have naturally sprung out of nothing and that all of life, with all of its perfectly aligned and intricately coordinated moving parts, that consciousness itself could have somehow magically sprung out of what British naturalist Charles Darwin referred to as a warm little pond.

The thesis that God exists as a supernatural force contains within it a mystery which is that the secrets of the universe, that which exists outside of nature, that which is a part of the mind of God, are aspects of existence that are mostly unknowable to man given that we are imperfect images of God and that we are, as such, granted only a limited degree of consciousness that corresponds with our frail physical and mental capability and life. That mystery of the meaning of life and the mysteries of the universe, and our limited capacity to perceive such mysteries, is inherent in the observable fact that man, unlike God the creator, cannot know everything and, as such, we cannot have perfect knowledge or consciousness. Our attempt to seize the opportunity to know everything, and to become, as such, gods, is well expressed in the biblical narrative of Adam and Eve and the temptation of the forbidden fruit. We thus hold a limited access to the greater mysteries of the universe and, as such, we are ultimately capable of grasping only a passing glimpse into the greater secrets of life and existence.

While we perceive that we are alive, we cannot fully know what this means or why we are alive. While we realize that we have vision when we open our eyes in the morning to a new day, we cannot really know or understand why we have vision or what causes vision beyond that which is knowable regarding the scientific mechanics of sight. We can only access a fraction of knowledge in terms of why the brain works the way it does. Like God, who is the creator of all things and who is, as such, the intelligent designer of the universe, we possess a free will to operate but in our limited capacity, which emanates from the fact that we are not God but rather that we are imperfect images of God, we can only operate within the realm which God created. Our free will provides us with the ability to make choices within the confines of circumstance, and our free will offers us the ability to accept or reject ideas and to choose to act upon ideas. Implicit in our ability to operate in the context of free will, Satan, the evil aspect, the dark angel, Lucifer, Mephistopheles, Beelzebub, Baphomet, will pry under our rafters and oil his way across the floor and into our minds.

I argue, with a metaphorical reliance on the Book of Genesis, that God created men and women in his image. A simple observance of nature indicates that God, a supernatural external force, created men and women equally but at the same time he created each differently from each other and differently from all other living beings on earth. Unlike all other living beings, God gave us consciousness and the ability to reason. We comprehend that we are alive, we comprehend the nature of existence, and we comprehend that we have a purpose in life beyond simply staying alive. We comprehend that we have a soul, a spiritual component, as evidenced by our ability to think and to assimilate knowledge, to reason, to create, to invent, to love, to hate, to imagine, to pray, to know right from wrong. That which separates us from other living beings, that which makes us images of God, is indeed our ability, albeit imperfect, to identify the nature of existence and the facts of reality.

Thus, we possess the ability to identify that which is real, and we are capable of understanding a great deal of that which is true by means of reason and by the use of language, both verbal and written, which is our primary means to identify and to affix names, symbols, and descriptions to all things that exist. We possess the ability to analyze and to assimilate the knowledge that we accumulate and to share knowledge with each other which has the dynamic effect of growing knowledge, and to build upon accumulated knowledge in order to create a better civilization while improving our own individual lives.

God created a world that includes the physical as well as the abstract and the spiritual. This becomes apparent when we observe with our senses that which is physical as well as when we observe, spiritually, as well as with our intellect and ability to reason, that which is conceptual. All living beings on earth, from man to the amoeba, experience emotion, attraction, attachment, we all possess the survival instinct and an ingrained fight or flight response. While human beings are emotional and instinctive beings, and while we share these same traits with other living beings, and while we react and respond to each other and our environment, we differ from each other and from other living beings in terms of our unique personal characteristics and our ability to temper our thoughts and emotions with judgement and discernment. We modify our instinctive and emotional response to internal and external stimuli with logic and with reason born out of propriety and self-interest.

Every human being, indeed, every living being and, for that matter, almost every essence and every element in the universe, whether alive or inanimate, holds various unique and different qualities, both within itself and amongst itself, with each essence and with each element different from every other thing. The Bible, which has become, and which remains, either directly or indirectly, the foundational document and the philosophical loadstone of civilization for both believers and nonbelievers provides a great metaphor to describe this phenomena in its creation narrative where God creates and then separates a series of things from himself and then from each other in order to create a balanced and interconnected world and universe. In this metaphor of creation, God created distinct elements and entities, each sharing complementary qualities with each other and each engaging with and reacting to other elements and entities in various ways. Thus, as examples, light cannot exist as an identifiable essence without interacting with darkness, heat cannot exist without interacting with cold, the earth cannot exist as an identifiable entity without interacting with the sky and the heavens.

Continuing on with the metaphor of Genesis, after creating men and women on the sixth day of creation, God then rested and reflected on the seventh day. This seventh day of rest symbolically marks, among other things, the creation of the means of measuring time and space. The twenty-four-hour cycle by which the earth rotates around the sun allows us to measure, to calculate and to differentiate the day and its place in time. The place of the earth as juxtaposed to the position of the sun and the planets allows us to measure and to differentiate space. The action and the energy that involves the rotation of the earth around the sun establishes the observable principle of energy as the motion of the earth is itself a reflection of the inherent nature of most things. As the Bible proceeds, and as mankind further identifies and names the various elements, the entities, and the living species, a greater level of identity emerges within man, one based upon his intellect, as man employs reason and consciousness as a means to increase the scientific and practical knowledge that is required to build and advance his civilization and to improve the quality and to expand the dimensions of human life.

Thus, conscious men and women, created as images of a God who is the source of consciousness, are capable of identifying and differentiating many of the various physical essences and entities that constitute the world. Men and women are also capable of identifying spiritual and moral concepts, also created by God, those being the *unalienable rights* as referred to by Thomas Jefferson, rights that are available to human conception through a cloudy and imperfect lens. We are capable of employing and harnessing the power of those rights to change our lives, to mold better societies, to create a better world. We are capable of perceiving and knowing a moral code which exists abstractly in nature and which is available to us as images of God who possess the ability to reason. We hold the ability to identify and discover that which is good and that which is evil, that which is right and that which is wrong.

So...then...what have we learned?

The nature of all living things holds a cyclical element as the world is tied to a cycle of the seasons and to the circle of life. This is true regarding the human being who is born, who dies and who cannot control certain aspects of his or her life and environment as we all live in a context of uncertainty and potential chaos. Yet, the spiritual component of men and women, that which makes us created in the image of God, that which grants us consciousness and a soul, that spiritual component means that by our ability to reason, by our intellect, by our education, by our choices, by our character and our faith, we are capable as individuals to control to a large extent the course of our lives and the direction of our destinies as well as the direction of our societies.

And, yet our ability to control and determine the direction of our lives and our destinies, as well as that of the collective destinies of the nations that we establish is predicated upon our knowledge of good and evil. As individuals, and collectively within society, we have obtained, and we will no doubt continue to obtain such knowledge through observation, trial and error, education, faith, prayer, and by means of intellectual growth. The course and the direction of our lives, and that of our organizations and our nations, are not predetermined but are rather determined by ideas and actions that we take in response to the ideas that we embrace within the context of both positive and negative situations and occurrences. Natural events both positive and negative, events that are outside of our control, these phenomena are known in the insurance industry as acts of god.

In that context, and using the Bible as a continuing metaphor, we have learned a great deal. We have learned, as previously mentioned, that if God, acting in the capacity as an outside supernatural force, created the universe and the world, that which he created is real and, as such, reality is real. We are capable of determining, with our senses, through our intellect, and through prayer and reflection, what is real and what is not real. We have learned that God gave man the ability to identify existence and reality by means of a spoken language which established the ability to reason, to integrate knowledge and to exchange ideas. We have learned, using the Book of Genesis as a metaphor, that God created men and women equally in his image. Out of that metaphor, we have derived what should be obvious which is that every single human life, every one of us, every image of God, is sacred and, as such, that every human life is worth living. The Talmud declared that every life is the equivalent of a universe. The destruction of a single human life, as such, constitutes the destruction of a universe.

And, yet, and this constitutes the great paradox of human existence, the pages of history as well as the story of our lives are, to varying degrees, often littered with horrendous examples of wickedness and sin, and with examples of evil rewarded in the material and temporal world. I shall further develop this question in the next chapter. Most nations, for example, were built upon variations of the ruins of war, pillage, confiscation, programs of collectivization, assassination, injustice, genocide, democide, all manner of the use of force and fraud or deception, with examples that are common and are too numerous to categorize. Many individuals of great wealth and power achieved their success through theft and deceptions which unjustly hurt or damaged others. Life is neither just, nor is life fair.

The Roman Catholic Church as well as various Protestant and Orthodox Christian churches and Judaism maintain a high standard regarding defining and defending each and every human life with doctrines that recognize that life begins at the moment of conception and ends at the moment of natural death. Indeed, this is why the church opposes abortion, infanticide, euthanasia, murder, suicide and the death penalty. Judaism maintains the standard that abortion, while not condoned, while strongly discouraged as immoral, and might be considered only with careful reasoning, is reluctantly permitted within the first 40 days after conception as this time-frame parallels the 40 years that the children of Israel wandered in the desert after obtaining freedom from bondage in Egypt. While there are great variations on this question within Islam, the general Muslim understanding is that the soul enters the fetus after 120 days. (2.)

The fundamental recognition that every human life is sui generis has resulted in a consensus, one that developed to varying degrees in all societies over several millennia, regarding prohibitions against murder, rape, torture, physical abuse, slavery, cannibalism and human sacrifice. This understanding is based upon the primary moral principle, as expressed in the Bible, that regards each and every human being as sacred and as created in God's image. This understanding has evolved over time and this principle has developed as a result of the accumulation of human experience, knowledge, science and education.

I would suggest, therefore, that we may detect the satanic influence within individuals as well as within philosophies, organizations, dogmas and doctrines that deliberately seek to undermine this principle. Ideas, philosophies and agendas that seek to undermine and, as such, to overthrow this abstract principle, as derived from divine law as it has been perceived by humanity for millennia, to uphold the value of every human life, represents the very embodiment of satanism. Indeed, the most fundamental and moral function of the nation-states that we establish, and the most basic purpose of the establishment of a separate system of justice, is to preserve and to uphold the principle of protecting the life of the citizen.

The Bible presents the metaphor of Adam and Eve as the first couple, the mother and the father of all of mankind, the genetic parents that many scientists call Y chromosome Adam and mitochondrial Eve. The metaphor of Adam and Eve presents the ideal sovereign social unit, the independent monogamous marriage of a man and a women. This recognition of the monogamous marriage between one man and one woman as the ideal human relationship, from a scientific as well as from a social and moral perspective, does not therefore de-legitimate or cancel the many and various alternative forms of family that have always existed.

The biblical creation metaphor describes the creation of a multitude of opposite essences and entities with each defining and each balancing the other. Simple observation indicates that there are natural elements that indicate an opposite nature of the male and the female with the obvious element being that each, while created equal, are biologically built in such a way as to interact with and complement the other. Beyond the biological reality of this observation, free will and social norms dictate the manner by which a man and a woman, as free will conscious individuals, might enter into that unique relationship with each other. The natural union of the man and the woman completes the life and the sense of purpose for each participant which is why every society in history has created meaningful and beautiful rituals that include levels of community involvement as a means to codify and to formalize the marriage commitment and to foster and nurture its success and continuation.

The institution of marriage, the married man and woman committed to each other, has proven to be the most natural and important social institution known to mankind in terms of regulating morality, checking and balancing excess and sin, fostering and advancing freedom and advancing the creativity and the individuality of each participant. Marriage, it should be noted, is by no means utopian as such relations may prove undesirable and untenable for certain individuals and for certain married couples.

Marriage is both a sacred covenant and a secular contract that is entered into as the best means of fostering children and developing an independent unit that has proven optimal in terms of developing material stability and wealth. The sexual act, which is unique to a man and a woman, is the re-enactment by human beings, imperfect images of God, of the creation of the universe by the perfect God. The sexual act which, biblically speaking, constitutes marriage in the literal sense is unique because, biologically speaking, the act of sexual intercourse holds the potential of producing a life which is the closest event by which human beings re-enact the creation of the world by God. The marriage also serves as a means of restraining one of the most powerful human urges known to man, the urge that cracks open the door to Satan, and that is the antinomian urge toward unbridled lust.

The marriage of a man and a woman established familial relations that developed over generations that would more broadly include the relationship of parents, siblings, the families of siblings, families in law, children, their families and their siblings and their in-law families. These relations would form the basis for the formation of the tribe which might develop, over time, customs, language and culture unique to the development of collective perceptions and experience. The tribe might, over time, gather amongst itself like minded families and affiliated tribes and this gathering may became the basis of the formation of the sovereign nation state. The Bible metaphorically expressed this principle as emanating from a God who originally separated essences and entities. The Bible further delineated the geographic location and the specific borders of each of the tribes that would constitute the federation of the children of Israel in Canaan and this development set the template for the eventual emergence of the nations of the world.

The Bible, which is further amplified and refined in Judaism by the Talmud, and in Christianity by the New Testament, as well as the works of numerous religious and scholarly philosophers, scientists, thinkers and intellectuals, offers a metaphor for the natural laws of nations and these biblical principles are, at their core, based upon an understanding that men and women, as imperfect images of God, are to approach their fellow men and their fellow women with the basic respect that should rightfully be afforded to any and all images of God. This principle was expressed by Rabbi Hillel the Elder and also by Jesus of Nazareth, who is referred to as the Christ by his followers.

Rabbi Hillel is attributed as having said: *If I am not for myself, who will be for me? And being only for myself, what am 'I'? And if not now, when?* (3.) and *"That which is hateful to you, do not do to your fellow.* (4.)

Jesus is attributed as having said in the Gospel of Matthew: *Teacher, which is the great commandment in the Law? And he said to him, You shall love the Lord your God with all your heart and with all your soul and with all your mind. This is the great and first commandment. And a second is like it: You shall love your neighbor as yourself. On these two commandments depend all the Law and the Prophets.* (5.)

WHO IS SATAN?

While Almighty God created the universe, and while God is good, the paradox that is embedded within this paradigm becomes manifest when evil holds sway in life and when evil is rewarded. Indeed, nature itself may visit evil upon human beings in the form of natural catastrophes such as earthquakes, volcanoes, fire, tsunamis, disease and pestilence. Evil may visit any one of us at any time in the form of a car crash, a structure falling off a building and hitting us on the head, a bad diagnosis from a doctor or any number of random freak accidents that may occur at any moment. A recent example of such an evil visitation is the suffering caused by the COVID-19 pandemic. While these phenomena constitute the normal risks associated with being alive and are, as such, a part of the natural cycle of life, the experience and the consequences, while not in the judgmental sense, may nevertheless be considered evil when we suffer from the ill effects. Indeed, it is particularly evil when an innocent child suffers from the scourge of cancer.

These realities, which are called Acts of God in insurance parlance, cause us to question the morality or even the existence of a loving God. There is ultimately no answer to such questions as to why bad things happen to good people as we cannot know the mind of God. Our obligation as human beings, an obligation that is reflected in the societies that we establish, is to try our best to protect ourselves from such dangers whenever possible and to mitigate catastrophe as best we can if and when it does occur. Indeed, in our limited capacity as mere human beings, we counter the effects of such evil phenomena with our desire to do good as we act, as individuals and through society, to invent and to develop various modalities that enhance safety and longevity by means of technologies such as the healing sciences and by numerous other means and disciplines to improve our safety. We do this instinctively as a means to protect our own lives and those of our loved ones.

Great success has accrued to individuals and to nations due to wrong-doing and evil. When God created men and women in his image, he did not re-create himself but, rather, he created imperfect beings who only get a glimpse at perfection. We slightly grasp the mind of God and the mysteries of the universe through a cloudy lens. The biblical metaphor of Adam and Eve partaking of the forbidden fruit and entering into a criminal pact with each other, a conspiracy against God, by trying to grab the golden ring of eternal knowledge resulted in their banishment from paradise. Ever since, we, their metaphorical ancestors, have wandered across the fruited plain of the earth seeking whatever solace and whatever meaning we might derive out of this veil of tears.

This is where Satan enters into the picture.

Satan does not exist in nature, per se, but Satan emerges out of the dark side of man's free will. Satan lurks in the shadows when good is absent. Satan, while hiding his countenance from man, will emerge when we refuse to recognize the good and when, even after we do recognize the good, we consciously and deliberately choose evil. Free will tempts us to take advantage of others, to violate the natural rights of others by means of force or deception in order to gain advantages for ourselves and this is likewise the case collectively when we employ our organizations and our nations toward evil intent and action. Indeed, the crowd, the mob, the collective, is more easily brought under the spell of Satan as the individual, when operating as part of a mob, is more likely to subsume the code of morality, of personal conscience and of independent thought in favor of the warm and comforting sensation of cheap acceptance and easy gain. Elements of individual sovereignty tend to be replaced by group-think and by group experience when the individual places him or herself at the service of the mob and by doing so, the individual compromises the faculty of objective reason which tends to be replaced by emotion and by excesses that are associated with the sensate.

The generation that established the American Republic in 1776 recognized the dangers associated with mob rule, a danger that they derisively referred to as Democracy. Thus, the American founders, as noted by John Adams, established a government of laws and not of men. In their genius, the American founders, drawing from enlightenment thought and practical experience, recognized the satanic element that is naturally embedded within mob rule and the dangers of allowing for the concentration of earthly power in the hands of the few. They recognized that evil is a normal human tendency which is why they established a government based upon the principles of a separation of powers, a system of checks and balances. By this means, the evil tendencies associated with both the mob and with the concentration of power, as ironically these two forces often work in tandem and with degrees of coordination, would be divided between competing political entities with each proscribed its own explicit powers and responsibilities.

We may be tempted to evil because evil is easy and, as such, evil is more immediate in terms of gratification. We may be tempted to evil because we believe there will be no consequence and simply because we can. The seven deadly sins, greed, envy, avarice and ambition spur us to commit unnatural acts when advantage may present itself. Pride causes us to develop an unrealistic and false sense of ourselves and, to the degree that we indulge pride, we become willing to uphold its scaffolding with lies and deceptions including those that we may internalize. Sloth and laziness tempt us to take shortcuts in order to achieve goals, shortcuts that may include dishonesty and deception. Lust and gluttony point us in the direction of over-indulging in the earthly pleasures. We develop individual character, forged by an escutcheon of truth, by means of identifying that which is true and, as such, that which is right and that which is good. Satan lurks within that which is false and that which is unnatural. We know, but yet we deny to ourselves, when we commit evil.

Why, then, are we so attracted to Satan?

Satan is not normal. Satan is not natural. Satan is not moral. To defy, or to subvert the normal, the natural, the moral, is to defy and to subvert our own minds and our own ability to reason, our intrinsic perception of morality and, as such, we subvert the order of the universe. We are all, I would contend, whether wittingly or unconsciously, attracted to the idea of subverting the normal, the natural, the moral. We all hold within us a deviant desire to subvert the laws of nature and to shake the cage of that which is normal. Indeed, in this sense, this tendency toward subversion, in and of itself, could be described as normal in that this tendency is, de facto, normal for us as human beings. We are attracted by that which is not rational and, as such, we are attracted by that which is not normal. Otherwise, we would be God.

The Bible has been interpreted to contain the principle that we are all sinners, a concept that has been described as emanating from the idea of original sin, as we all struggle with this irrational and immoral side of our nature. This tendency, which is both a byproduct of and which is the mirror opposite to reason and by which we subvert our natural sense of morality is as much an element that separates humanity from all other living beings as is consciousness and reason itself. The entire narrative of every human life, and every society, is to push back against, to restrain, to regulate, to identify and to oppose that tendency and, in the broad sense, this is the key purpose, or I should say this should be the key purpose, of the organizations and the nations that we establish.

THE JEWISH CONCEPTION OF SATAN

The Jewish understanding of Satan, as opposed to the more literal anthropomorphic Christian conception of Satan, and while noting that each conception has influenced and has intersected with the other, is that the Jewish Satan is the yetzer hara, the evil inclination. An evil inclination, as such, does not contradict the oneness of the all-knowing God but, rather, the yetzer hara emanates from denying God, denying objective and created truths and, more broadly, rejecting the natural order of the universe. Satan enters into the picture when we deny abstract truths, when we reject what the ancient Greeks called Logos. As imperfect images of God, we are not capable of fully knowing the entirety of God and of all of that which is true. We thus tend to deny God and turn to Satan because doing so is cheap and easy. With Satan we can pretend to create our own truths as we justify anything to suit our desires. It is easy to deny reality and to disconnect from the moral code created by God. By such denial we seize gratification from excessively partaking in otherwise legitimate pleasures as well as illicit pleasures. This becomes an overall part of corruption and a usurpation of powers.

Judaism is a faith that is based upon divine revelation and this revelation centers upon the climactic and pivotal events of Sinai where God handed to the children of Israel, by means of his humble prophet Moses, a blueprint for how to understand that which is real and that which is right. At Sinai, the Israelites received a constitution that would be interpreted and applied by priests and sages in every generation going forward. The Torah of Sinai established the goal-posts in terms of how mankind, with an extra set of rules for the Israelites, might properly partake in the earthly pleasures of creation while retaining and while advancing individual freedom and the moral order. God asked the Israelites to assume an extra layer of responsibility so they could know God, partner with God, witness to God, and serve God and, by doing so, serve as an example and, as such, as a light unto the nations of the world.

Christianity is also a faith that is based upon what is believed by its adherents to be divine revelation by God who came to earth in the form of a man, Jesus, who Christians call the Christ. Jesus ministry fully embraced the moral and ethical precepts of the revelations of Sinai, as contained within the Torah, with additional insights and revelations that would form the basis of the acceptance of the Sinaitic revelations for his followers who would proceed to synthesize that revelation with the knowledge of the Greeks and the Romans. That synthesis would establish the progressive Christian churches which would provide the foundation of western civilization. Christianity brought to the world at large a moral code that would lead toward the eventual abolition of human sacrifice, slavery, infanticide and torture. When Jesus stood up against Pontius Pilate, who represented the secular power of Rome, the most powerful empire on earth at the time, and announced that he answered to a higher authority, he advanced the principle that the individual derives his sovereignty from God and not from the man-made state. Jesus action, which directly led to his brutal crucifixion a short time later, has inspired freedom-loving people ever since.

Islam is also a faith that is based upon revelation in the form of a written dialogue, known as the Koran, which tradition holds consists of the narrative between Muhammad, who is referred to by his followers as the last Prophet, and the angel Gabriel. Many other religions, including many animist and indigenous faiths around the world as well as more modern religions such as Mormonism and Bahai, were also founded by leaders who claimed to have received divine revelation. While none of these religions, including Judaism and Christianity, are anywhere near perfect as, by their own doctrine, only God is perfect. They have all been subject to imperfect interpretations of revelation and other admixtures by fallible people. Each faith can nevertheless be judged based upon the moral code they impart and upon their own merits based upon objective measurements of reason.

Conversely, religious and non-religious systems of belief hold satanic principles that involve an equal and unregulated distribution of a claim to personal revelatory experience. As such, the satanic idea holds that every human being is either a god or is an enlightened superior being who holds messianic and personal access to the divine and to revelation. The satanic idea is not to know God and, as such, to not accept elements of creation and revelation by means of learning and prayer but, rather, the satanic believer pretends that he is god. He feels justified when he attempts, often in combination with fellow adherents who are equally intoxicated and deluded by this same satanic principle, to seize power over others as a means to reinvent the universe and to pretend to create a perfected world.

The God-fearing believer, on the other hand, seeks to change the world for the better by changing himself, by knowing truths through education, through hard work and prayer, and by applying those truths to improve his own life as well as toward improving the direction of his society. I should note that various atheistic oriented religions, such as Unitarian-Universalism, or Reconstructionist Judaism, or various permutations of eastern religions are not necessarily satanic per se. While the satanic principle tends to be an active, if not hidden, principle of belief, generally atheistic and secular religions and organizations appear to be passive or agnostic and, as such, they are based upon a tendency toward unbelief in anything beyond the material universe. It is also true, I would hasten to note, that various deeply religious and God-fearing cults have been and continue to be imbued by, and I would suggest corrupted by the satanic principle as would be the case, for example, with such groups as al-Qaeda and ISIS.

The great contribution of Judaism to human progress was the realization that a supernatural objective force, one that we call God, exists outside the natural universe, a universe that was created by that same force. In this sense, the Jew came to believe that there was a higher power and, as such, that there was a higher purpose to life than that which is detectable in the natural world. The great struggle of the ancient Israelites is represented by the golden calf at the foot of Sinai, the lowest and the most degraded event in Jewish history, an event that was simultaneously juxtaposed with the most exalted event, Moses receiving the Torah from God at the top of Sinai. This struggle continues today within the individual Jew and within the Jewish people acting as a microcosm for all of mankind. This struggle is between belief in God and belief in the adversary, the satanic influence that captivates and enthralls Man. The adversary draws man and the societies that he establishes away from truths and away from faith.

The generations from Sinai to the Babylonian captivity struggled with the satanic influence as represented by idol worship, the worship of inanimate objects allegedly infused with magical powers by elites who controlled the surrounding tribes and empires. After the return from Babylonian exile and after coming home to Judaea, where the Jews re-established their commonwealth, satanic temptations tended to manifest in the form of certain elements of external Hellenic influence and an internal civil war that was often driven by petty ambition and manipulation.

A significant portion of 17th Century Judaism would fall under the satanic sway of a movement that was led by an antinomian false messiah from Ottoman Turkish Smyrna by the name of Sabbatai Zevi who unleashed a call for the overthrow of the laws of the Torah and, as such, for the overthrow of Judaism. Zevi's methodology was to deliberately and publicly desecrate and pervert the Torah under the guise that such desecration would lead mankind toward a level of depravity which would cause the messiah to come to the rescue and launch a perfected messianic age. Sabbatai Zvai's utopian movement embraced an earthly collectivist and communistic vision that would seek to abolish the institutions that were derived from nature and natures God including property, the nation-state, faith in God, Marriage, and an objective understanding of a moral code and of reality itself. Indeed, Zvai's movement would eventually mirror that of the 18th Century Illuminati which would, in turn, influenced the Reign of Terror that co-opted the otherwise pro-American French Revolution. This satanic antinomian movement would later find resonance in the emergence of the two great and highly secretive socialist experiments that bore fruit in the 20th Century, Communism and Nazism.

Sabbatai Zevi's ideas, as spearheaded by his charismatic appearance and by his cult of personality, embraced many forms and practices of the occultic movements that have always bubbled just below the surface of western society. In the occultic significant year of 1666, Sabbatai Zvai directly and personally challenged the authority of the Ottoman Sultan in Constantinople. Zvai backed down after staring down the Sultan who offered him conversion to Islam or execution. He spent the remainder of his life under house arrest as a local satrap in Ottoman Albania. The craze that he launched in many Jewish communities in Europe collapsed in disarray and disillusionment.

Yet the movement that Sabbatai Zevi launched, a movement that is known to history as the Sabbatian movement, would continue to endure underground where it was embraced by elements of the Jewish elite and where it would develop secret societies and its own symbols and code language. This development was part of a pattern that was not new or unique in history as satanic movements, as illustrated, have always shielded themselves from public view due to their un-natural and, as such, their un-popular agendas as public exposure reveals their subversive methods which damages their ability to function. While various respectable conspiracy researchers have often linked Sabbateanism, and its offshoot, Frankism, a movement that was launched by a protégé of Sabbatai Zevi, the Polish rag merchant Jacob Frank, to the Young Turk movement that overthrew the Ottoman Turkish Sultanate and to the founding of the Reform and Conservative movements in Judaism, it is ultimately impossible to know for sure if this is true as, we should note, the Sabbatian and the Frankest movements were secret and, as such, their various machinations were, and probably still are, carried out in secret.

The experience of the ancient Israelites at Mount Sinai marked the pivotal point at which the Israelites accepted divine revelation and began to strive toward understanding the intricacies of what they perceived to be the laws of God both in terms of outward practice and in terms of morals and ethics. Certain laws would apply exclusively to the Israelites as means to advance their holiness, laws such as kosher dietary laws, ritual slaughter, and a labyrinthine web of various laws and practices that were meant to separate the Israelite nation and Israelite life from that of other nations. The Torah describes this idea in Leviticus: *You shall be holy because I am holy.* (6.) Ritual laws and customs would also emerge in other nations and these laws and customs would also serve the same purpose in many of those great nations and cultures.

At Mount Sinai, Israel received the moral and ethical code for all of mankind including a ban on murder and theft. This meant respect for the integrity, the inherent worth and the natural rights of every individual human being. The admonition against theft established the principle of private property. The admonition against bearing false witness established the principle of telling the truth with the implied command to expose falsehood and to not use the name of God in vain. The Israelite would not stand by the blood of his brother which established the principle of Justice. Other commands that would emanate from Sinai would include a ban on revenge, which implies forgiveness, mercy, leniency and reparation, and a command to love your neighbor as yourself.

At Mount Sinai, with Moses serving as the agent for mankind, God commanded all of mankind to engage in good deeds and to conduct acts of charity and kindness as the ultimate virtue. Leviticus records: *When you reap your harvest, leave the corners of your field for the poor.* (7.) *When you pluck the grapes in your vineyard, leave those grapes that fall for the poor and for the stranger.* (8.)

From the time of idol worship to the time of Sabbatai Zevi, to the present time, the Jewish people have struggled with the yetzer hara, the evil inclination and yet, clearly, the covenant between God and Israel and, more broadly, the logical and the faithful covenant between God and man remains intact and remains unchanged.

THE NEW-AGE SATAN

Satan represents sin and sin, in human terms, represents a corruption of the good and, as such, a corruption of the natural order. Conscious man, the image of God, seeks limited individual rights and sovereignty under God, the great sovereign, and, in that context, man seeks a maximum degree of autonomy over his own life and over his own destiny. Man conducts his affairs by establishing personal and professional relations and associations and, in the macrocosmic sense, man establishes governments as a means to preserve, protect and defend his own natural rights and to protect the rights of the weaker members of his society. Man protects such rights against intrigue and what I would describe as a permanent and ongoing conspiracy to usurp and subvert those rights and to subvert the natural order. This conspiracy represents the satanic influence, which is comparable, in mathematical terms, to the relationship between positive and negative numbers. Negative numbers are a measurement of quantities that are less than zero and are less than nothing, and yet, negative numbers are, nevertheless, a real expression of value.

The satanic influence represents an inversion and a perversion of the good as good is defined by nature and reason. While all human beings are tempted by sin, as a sinful aspect of our natures appear to be baked into who we are, we nevertheless instinctively know what sin is when we see sin and we know when we choose sin even when we try to conceal that knowledge from ourselves. Indeed, most major decisions that we make involve varying degrees of identifying, weighing, measuring, judging and choosing various and at times complex elements and aspects of both virtue and sin.

Given that Satan is un-natural and, if you will, Satan is un-Godly, Satanism, as such, has always lurked in the shadows. Satan must be hidden from view as exposure to the truth of daylight dissipates its powers. We struggle with Satan as we hide Satan even from ourselves as we deny Satan when Satan manifests in broad daylight and within our midst. Because Satan is un-natural, we are repelled from Satan and, as such, we would rather not acknowledge

Satan even when Satan appears right under our noses. As the saying goes, the left hand does not always know what the right hand is doing. Exposure leaves the endeavors of Satan vulnerable to collapse and failure. On a microcosmic level, the influence of Satan might become manifested by, as examples, an individual exposed for having embezzled funds from his employer or the exposure of a person or a group having bribed a government official in exchange for a favor.

Grave dangers may result from secrecy when secrecy predominates within a small group of people such as a family, or within larger organizations such as corporations, or within government agencies such as the CIA, or within secret societies or secret fraternities. Clearly certain groups were established with the express purpose of maintaining secrecy as a means to subvert order by committing crimes such as those who plot to rob a bank or a Mafia syndicate or a Narco-Terrorist Cartel. While secrecy, by nature, can be and often is vulnerable to the deceptive forces of satanic influence, secrecy itself, paradoxically, is necessary for freedom and is a basic human right. We possess a natural right to privacy and confidentiality as codified by certain relationships such as marriage, professional relationships such as lawyer-client privilege, and religious relationships such as discourse between a pastor and a congregant or a priest and a confessor. Companies have a right, for example, to expect employees to sign a confidentiality agreement as there is an element of secrecy that is inherent within property and propriety.

And yet, I would argue, the natural tendency toward corruption that emanates from secrecy, when not checked by investigation and by an independent system of justice, may become enthroned and, as such, may become the established norm over time. The establishment of corrupt satanic principles may go beyond the merely negative machinations of an individual, or a culture of corruption or of wrongdoing, or the occasional fib or slip-up, or an organization that might become mired in bad habits or bad mores. The emergence of a satanic establishment, I would argue, represents a grand conspiracy that goes back to ancient times, one that has been informally passed on and one that has been perpetrated in every generation ever since. This is a conspiracy that constitutes a specter that haunts us today.

Whittaker Chambers was an American Communist spy who, while working on behalf of Josef Stalin, managed the secret activities of his fellow travelers hidden within the ranks of the administration of Franklin D. Roosevelt in the 1930's. Chambers had a change of heart in the late 1930's due to his having become a Christian. The final straw for Chambers, causing his complete break with Communism, was the Hitler-Stalin Pact of August 9, 1939 as this singular event signaled to him that the high-level officials that he had previously managed for Stalin were now working for Adolf Hitler as well. He quite reasonably concluded that his country was in grave danger as a result of that pact which precipitated the invasion of Poland by the Nazis and the Soviets and which launched World War II. This event led Chambers to famously blow the whistle on such officials as Under Secretary of State Alger Hiss and Under Secretary of the Treasury Harry Dexter White among others.

In his autobiography, Witness, Whittaker Chambers described this grand conspiracy to which I refer as a conspiracy of gentlemen. (9.) By this, Chambers meant that the Communists, and their vast and international apparatus were not necessarily meeting and plotting in some proverbial smoked filled room. The Communist conspiracy to overthrow the social order, which consisted of a fully witting and interlocking international core of tightly knit cadres, concentric rings of semi-witting fellow traveler groups and a diverse basket of largely unwitting camp followers, included informal networks of interlocking people and groups who generally thought and acted alike. A certain segment of that group, those to whom V. I. Lenin referred to as useful idiots, were not conscious or aware, or they were perhaps partially conscious of what they were doing or why they believed what they believed. The lure of social acceptance and the convenience of group-think swept away reason and rational solutions to social problems as the followers became duped by empty platitudes and bumper-sticker slogans that had no actual meaning but offered a sense of holier than thou righteousness and a warm fuzzy feeling. Many of these camp followers had been taken in by a sophisticated propaganda campaign that was conducted, at its core, by the witting and conscious Communist core of cadres.

This does not mean that the Communists got along well with each other as, quite the contrary, the normal rivalries that accompany ambition, greed, power, material wealth, control, would wrack havoc upon the Communist apparatus leading to assassinations and in many cases to war. Chambers wrote that the Communist conspiracy consisted of an unholy alliance between wealthy segments of society and elements of the poorest which were dependent on the wealthy benefactors. (10.) This grand conspiracy operated in secret and its participants consciously and unwittingly embraced and manipulated the various tools of the satanic principle.

The New Age is a modern reference to an ancient set of beliefs or, more accurately, a set of non-beliefs that have always claimed to oppose the establishment beliefs of their times. As mankind has progressed through the pages of human history, man has grown in consciousness regarding his true nature. Man has, as a result of experience, developed a growing awareness, due to the expansion of his knowledge, learning, culture and interaction, of his own individual sovereignty under God as the ultimate source of sovereignty. In response to this growing knowledge, man has gradually but inexorably moved in the direction of rejecting ancient collectivist societies, those to which British industrialist Frederic Engels referred to as primitive socialism, in favor of more progressive societies that enfranchise the rights and the sovereignty of the individual. Man has established modes of governance that protect his natural rights and the rights of his most vulnerable fellows, forms of governance that check and balance his dark and corrupt impulses by distributing governing powers.

The New Age Movement has been marketed by its advocates as a challenge to the establishment, yet the truth is the exact opposite. They glom onto genuine organic movements that seek enfranchisement and, in a manner similar to the tactics of the communists, they infiltrate those movements and, simultaneously, they corrupt the establishment which might react, to varying degrees, to those movements. The tools subversively employed in the development of a dialectical conflict are meant to preserve collectivism and control and to do the opposite of what appears to be the case on the surface as they seek to weaken enfranchisement. The New Age promotes dangerous antinomian and anarchic tendencies that exist within all of us and within our societies. They seek to overthrow the moral order by weakening and undermining the individual, the autonomous family, the tribe, the association, the nation-state, property, business, education, independent systems of justice and organized faith. The New Age bifurcates consciousness by claiming that while that which is real is not really real, on the other hand the unknown, the mystery religion, the occult, is actually real but is not knowable or accessible to anyone other than a select cabal of superior elites.

The New Age occult is the modern variation of the ancient idol-worshipping cult that existed with variations in every ancient society. This was the very phenomena that the Bible warns us about. Idol-worship was a state-run institution by which the state, usually headed up by a god-king, claimed to control the secrets of the universe and pretended to engage in farcical forms of magic. We know from history that these claims to control mystical knowledge were based upon a lie. In order to perpetrate that lie, and in order to consolidate earthly powers, a ruling elite operated as a state-controlled monopolistic secret society with totalitarian police power.

The parallels between the ancient idol-worshipping cults and the elitist New Age of today is easily discernable and is obvious to anyone with eyes ears and a brain. The ancient idol-worshipping cult imposed its belief system on its population using tools such as terror, mind control techniques and total control over the means of communication. They were satanic in that they sought to overturn God and nature by force and by subversion. They sought to replace the sovereignty and the integrity of the man and the woman created in the image of God by attempting to turn their fellow human beings into a collectivist mass of mind-controlled robots or what might today be called human resources. They attempted to abolish the natural right to property with the gathering of all material resources into their own hands by means of monopoly, currency manipulation and confiscation. By setting up a false god, they attempted to control and define morality in a manner that would weaken consciousness and independence by promoting sexual vice and by other means to break down the natural and independent institution of the sovereign family.

The New Age occult, which by its own definition is secretive as it is based upon the false premise that a select few have access to secret mystical knowledge that they believe makes them superior, is the de-facto religion of elites around the world and this has always been true going back in history since day one. The believers in this faith derive a moral sense of justification to wield power over nations and over peoples in the name of implementing their so-called enlightened ideas. This is why the occult elites have been able to feel moral about carrying out holocausts, genocides, planned famines and pandemics, world wars, population control experiments and other programs of social engineering. They are, after all, god and as such they are, after all, the authors of morality and of reality itself.

While the occult is a satanic idea that is embraced by those at the highest levels of power in government, business, culture and even in religion, and while they generally operate in secret, as they will often display the outward trappings of normality and modesty, and while many of them may even have deluded themselves in this regard, there has nevertheless also been an open occult religion, one that runs like a threat through history. I argue that both the open and the secret, the witting and the unwitting elements of the occult, constitute an informal and satanic conspiracy against God, against nature and against mankind.

THE SATANIC CONSPIRACY

The satanic conspiracy received its first major blow in human history at Mount Sinai when the Lord God, King of the Universe, revealed the law to all of mankind through Moses. The Israelites would go on to struggle to know God and to live by God's revealed laws and, as such, to strive to become a light of truth unto the nations and peoples of the world. The satanic conspiracy received its second major blow on a worldwide scale through the ministry of Jesus which carried forth the laws of God, as revealed at Mount Sinai and, as such, the laws of truth to the far corners of the world.

The knowledge of God, and the advancement of a better understanding of the natural rights of the images of God, which is the sovereign man and woman under God, and the knowledge of the truth of God's creation in its physical as well as in its abstract form would challenge the ancient conspiracy against God, the worship of the false graven image set up by the authoritarian state and the worship of the god-king who claimed to be the source of creation and truth. A significant point of demarcation in terms of defeating the conspiracy was the 312 CE victory of Roman general Constantine at Milvian Bridge which he attributed to divine intervention. This marked the Christian era in Rome. Christianity would subsequently spread across Europe and the New World. It should be noted that Christianity had spread rapidly, and out in the open, across Roman realms in the centuries leading up to Constantine. Christianity involves a personal and voluntary bond between the conscious individual and God with Jesus acting as intercessor.

The satanic conspiracy went underground after Constantine established Christianity as the religion of the Roman Empire and it remains mostly underground to this day. Occultic mystery cults have always sprung up and have often bubbled just below the surface of western society where they have at times held sway in corrupt ways, but it was not until the 18th Century that satanic occultism became more organized and became more influential amongst elite circles. This occurred as a result of the establishment of freemasonic lodges and, on May 1, 1776, the establishment of the Bavarian Illuminati by Ingolstadt University Professor Adam Weishaupt.

The doctrines of the Illuminati, the study of which is part of standard mainstream history in Europe, but which is viewed with suspicion in America, are, I argue, satanic in nature. The Illuminati effectively re-established the principle of world order which had been the doctrine of pre-Christian Rome which sought a one world utopian government under the rule of an Emperor god. The Illuminati, which sought the collapse of all religions and the folding of the nation-state into a solitary world authority run by an enlightened elect, operated in secret and subversively knowing full well that the exposure of their diabolical scheme would destroy their chances for success.

Adam Weishaupt sought to accomplish this agenda by infiltrating the already existing and generally Christian and patriotic Masonic Lodges of Europe with the goal of developing an inner illuminated core of Illuminatus initiates within those secret societies. One great historic late 18th Century work documenting the activities and influence of the Illuminati is *Proofs of a Conspiracy: Against all the Religions and Governments of Europe, carried on in the secret meetings of Freemasons, Illuminati, and Reading Societies* by Scottish physicist, mathematician and University of Edinburgh Professor John Robison. (11.)   Another great work, one which connects the Illuminati with the development of the French Jacobin societies that would inspire the French Reign of Terror, 1793-1795, was written by French Jesuit Priest Abbe Agustin Barruel, who authored *Memoirs Illustrating the History of Jacobinism.* (12.)

I am not prepared to suggest that all Masonic Lodges are infiltrated by the Illuminati, nor do I suggest that Masonry is in and of itself satanic as, I assume, God fearing secret societies that are made up of God-fearing men and women have always existed and will continue to exist. Indeed, I would argue, patriotic secret societies established on masonic lines played a major and positive role in American history. The Sons of Liberty, for example, was essentially a masonic lodge that plotted the 1773 Boston Tea Party, the primary event triggering the 1776 American Declaration of

Independence. Most of the American founding fathers, including George Washington and Benjamin Franklin, were Christians and masons and masonry influenced the creation of the Great Seal of the United States as well as the architectural blueprint for Washington, D. C.

George Washington was, however, fully aware of the dangers posed by secretive occultic and satanic Illuminated Masonic Lodges. On October 2, 1798, Maryland Minister George William Snyder sent a copy of Robison's book *Proofs of a Conspiracy* to retired President George Washington. In his accompanying letter to Washington, Snyder wrote:

It was some Time since that a Book fell into my Hands entitled "Proofs of a Conspiracy &c. by John Robison," which gives a full Account of a Society of Freemasons, that distinguishes itself by the Name "of Illuminati," whose Plan is to overturn all Government and all Religion, even natural; and who endeavor to eradicate every Idea of a Supreme Being and distinguish Man from Beast by his Shape only. A Thought suggested itself to me, that some of the Lodges in the United States might have caught the Infection and might cooperate with the Illuminati or the Jacobine Club in France. (13.)

Washington replied on September 25:

I have heard much of the nefarious, & dangerous plan, & doctrines of the Illuminati... except to correct an error you have run into, of my Presiding over the English lodges in this Country. The fact is, I preside over none, nor have I been in one more than once or twice, within the last thirty years. I believe, notwithstanding, that none of the Lodges in this Country are contaminated with the principles ascribed to the Society of the Illuminati.

As president, Washington had denounced the so-called Democratic Societies, blaming them for instigating the Whiskey Rebellion in western Pennsylvania. Washington wrote:

It was not my intention to doubt that the Doctrines of the Illuminati, and principles of Jacobinism had not spread in the

United States. On the contrary, no one is more fully satisfied of this fact than I am.

The idea I meant to convey, was, that I did not believe that the Lodges of Free Masons in this Country had, as Societies, endeavored to propagate the diabolical tenets of the first, or the pernicious principles of the latter (if they are susceptible of separation). That Individuals of them may have done it, and that the founder, or instrument employed to found, the Democratic Societies in the United States, may have had these objects—and actually had a separation of the People from their Government in view, is too evident to be questioned. (14.)

On April 27, 1961, speaking before the America Newspaper Publishers Association at the Waldorf Astoria Hotel, President John F. Kennedy stated:

The very word "secrecy" is repugnant in a free and open society; and we are as a people inherently and historically opposed to secret societies, to secret oaths and to secret proceedings. We decided long ago that the dangers of excessive and unwarranted concealment of pertinent facts far outweighed the dangers which are cited to justify it. Even today, there is little value in opposing the threat of a closed society by imitating its arbitrary restrictions. Even today, there is little value in insuring the survival of our nation if our traditions do not survive with it. And there is very grave danger that an announced need for increased security will be seized upon by those anxious to expand its meaning to the very limits of official censorship and concealment. That I do not intend to permit to the extent that it is in my control. And no official of my Administration, whether his rank is high or low, civilian or military, should interpret my words here tonight as an excuse to censor the news, to stifle dissent, to cover up our mistakes or to withhold from the press and the public the facts they deserve to know. (15.)

President Kennedy thus identified the inherent dangers that are naturally associated with the existence of secret societies where members swear secret oaths and engage in secret proceedings. I should note, for the record, that I have never personally taken any oath to any society as the only oaths that I have ever personally sworn is a pledge of allegiance to the flag of the United States of America and my pledge of marriage to my wife at the time of our wedding. To swear an oath of loyalty to a secret society, particularly one that is as vast, as interconnected and as international as is Freemasonry, is problematic on many levels to put it mildly. A brief study of the Masonic Oath, an oath which is fairly standardized for all Masonic lodges around the world, indicates that the initiate is placing his loyalty to Masonry over that of his own country and even over his own wife and family.

It appears obvious to me that such an oath to a secret society presents a major conflict of interest for a politician, for example, who would be required to take an oath of office or a Judge who is supposed to impartially preside over a case. Technically, perhaps, a president of the United States would hold his oath to Masonry and to his fellow Masons first over that of his oath to serve his country. What happens, for example, if a Masonic Judge has before him a fellow Mason who might be appearing as a defendant? Would he offer his fellow initiate more lenient treatment than he might offer a non-initiate? Policemen form fraternal organizations that are modelled on masonic lines. Might a policeman who has sworn a masonic oath to his benevolent association, for example, turn in a fellow policeman who might have also taken that same oath in a criminal matter or would the initiate be expected to protect his fellow initiate first, before the interests of his mission as a police officer, in a case that might involve criminal conduct?

The Masonic Oath is revealing as versions of this type of oath are likely taken by the initiates of most secret societies around the world. The oath is as follows:

I --- do hereby and hereon most solemnly and sincerely promise and swear, that I will hail, ever conceal, and never reveal any of the secrets, arts, parts, point or points, of the Master Mason's Degree, to any person or persons whomsoever, except that it be a true and lawful brother of this Degree. (16.)

...Further, that I will keep a worthy brother Master Mason's secrets inviolable, when communicated to and received by me as such, murder and treason excepted.

...All this I most solemnly, sincerely promise and swear, with a firm and steady resolution to perform the same, without any hesitation, myself, under no less penalty than that of having my body severed in two, my bowels taken from thence and burned to ashes, the ashes scattered before the four winds of heaven, that no more remembrance might be had of so vile and wicked a wretch as I would be, should I ever, knowingly, violate this my Master Mason's obligation. (17.)

In that same seminal speech to the American Newspaper Publishers Association, President Kennedy identified that which he explicitly called a conspiracy, an identification that remains as relevant today as it was when he issued those remarks which, some conspiracy theorists have speculated, might have contributed to his eventual and untimely assassination. John F. Kennedy alluded to a solution to the problem of secret societies:

It requires a change in outlook, a change in tactics, a change in missions--by the government, by the people, by every businessman or labor leader, and by every newspaper. For we are opposed around the world by a monolithic and ruthless conspiracy that relies primarily on covert means for expanding its sphere of influence--on infiltration instead of invasion, on subversion instead of elections, on intimidation instead of free choice, on guerrillas by night instead of armies by day. It is a system which has conscripted vast human and material resources into the building of a tightly knit, highly efficient machine that combines military, diplomatic, intelligence, economic, scientific and political operations.

Its preparations are concealed, not published. Its mistakes are buried, not headlined. Its dissenters are silenced, not praised. No expenditure is questioned, no rumor is printed, no secret is revealed. It conducts the Cold War, in short, with a war-time discipline no democracy would ever hope or wish to match. (18.)

To recap, the Satanic conspiracy involves a satanic clique seeking control over others, over societies and ultimately over the world. The Satanist feels insecure in his person and he feels fearful over facing the uncertainties and the imperfections of life, so he seeks to change and to control human nature by means of exercising overt as well as covert power. The Satanist seeks to become God and, as such, to overthrow God and nature by controlling the world. Individuals and nations do evil things as human nature has an evil side. The best method for reducing those tendencies and activities, which exist within us and within the societies that we create, besides the obvious, which is faith in God and a quest for truth, is the conscious development by rational man of a system of checks and balances. By this means we are better able to restrain negative tendencies so as to prevent too much power from falling into the hands of a few at any given time.

For this reason, the Satanic Conspiracy seeks to monopolize power by dominating several natural nexuses of power. Those areas include politics, money, communication, science, culture, academia and religion. The Satanic Conspiracy, after millennia of clandestine advancement and successes gained by their conspiracy to diminish the natural powers of the conscious sovereign individual under God, has now thoroughly infiltrated all of those areas and, as a result, the Satanic Conspiracy now holds the upper hand in many respects.

In politics, the Satanic Conspiracy is active, in the macrocosmic sense, whenever we witness tendencies toward global governance. While conflict and war are at times inevitable and while wars may be unavoidable, I would suggest that a high degree of satanic planning resided at the core of the big and destructive genocidal wars of the past half millennia. Those wars were engineered and enhanced as means to bring about world conquest and world order either through the old-fashioned imperialistic colonial methods of military conquest or by means of weakening social order through terror which shatters conventional modes and structures supporting public morality. The satanic Illuminati of 1776 gave birth, by means of the machinations of a web of Parisian secret societies, to the French Reign of Terror which constituted the world's first Communist coup d'état. The 1793 Reign of Terror sought to undo the American inspired French Revolution of 1789, a popular revolution that sought to empower the individual by peacefully establishing a constitutional monarchy and a National Assembly. The satanic Reign of Terror gave birth to the slogan that was hatched within those secret societies: *Liberty, Fraternity, Equality.* The concept of Fraternity eventually gave birth to Fascism and Nazism and the concept of Equality eventually manifested as Communism. (19.)

The Satanic Conspiracy of today is not attempting to instigate wholesale war and, while this might change, the conspiracy now embraces tactics of gradualism by means of promoting fearful conspiracy theories and by tightening the grip on the world by means of technology. Much debate surrounded whether or not the 1967 publication *The Report from Iron Mountain* was authentic but, either way, and the denials of its authenticity appear sketchy, this book, the contributors of which included such doyens of the establishment as Harvard Economist John Kenneth Galbraith, offers insights into how the satanic establishment plans to manipulate and mass-control the minds and the politics of the god-fearing sovereign citizen. (20.)

The Report from Iron Mountain claimed that a 15-member panel of experts, a so-called Special Study Group, set up in 1963, examined potential problems that might arise for the world order agenda if peace, God forbid, was to break out around the world. The thinking here was similar to that revealed by the 1952-1954 Reese Committee Report which documented notes from a 1911 study that had been issued by the Carnegie Endowment for International Peace, a study that concluded, a few years before the outbreak of World War I, that the best way to advance the agenda of world socialism was by means of total war. (21.) *The Report from Iron Mountain* had similarly concluded that if peace *could be achieved, it would almost certainly not be in the best interests of society to achieve it.* Iron Mountain stated: *War was a part of the economy. Therefore, it was necessary to conceive a state of war for a stable economy.* (22.)

The Report from Iron Mountain must have been written by a Prophet, or perhaps, if you will, written by an anti-Prophet in that it recommended *credible substitutes,* and paying a *blood price* as a means to emulate the economic and perhaps the political functions of war. The report recommended introducing credible reports, or what we might more accurately call propaganda, regarding alien *life-forms* and to create a *euphemized form* of slavery *consistent with modern technology and political processes.* We are now hearing reports of credible claims of alleged sightings of alien spaceships. Various establishment figures, such as former Israeli defense official Haim Eshed and former President Barack Obama have recently at least implied that they are aware of secret government contact with extraterrestrials. (23.)

What exactly did the authors of *The Report from Iron Mountain* mean by a *euphemized form* of slavery? What comes to mind is a comment that was made by Aldous Huxley, author of Brave New World and brother of Julian Huxley who was the founder of UNESCO, when he stated in an interview that he gave shortly before his LSD induced and filmed suicide on November 22, 1963:

There will be, in the next generation or so, a pharmacological method of making people love their servitude, and producing dictatorship without tears, so to speak, producing a kind of painless concentration camp for entire societies, so that people will in fact have their liberties taken away from them, but will rather enjoy it, because they will be distracted from any desire to rebel by propaganda or brainwashing, or brainwashing enhanced by pharmacological methods. And this seems to be the final revolution.
(24.)

The Report from Iron Mountain further noted that a method of propaganda that might be employed by this nebulous establishment in terms of scaring the world into surrendering sovereignty and sovereign individual rights would be *particularly promising in gaining the attention of the malleable masses* and that would be the threat of *gross pollution of the environment.* This certainly rings a bell, does it not? I recall various scares starting in the late 1960's with *The Population Bomb* by Paul and Anne Ehrlich, which predicted massive famine and social unrest across the world due to over-population, then there was the unexplained oxygen depleting ozone hole, than there was Chlorofluorocarbons causing the oceans and the lakes to become too acidic to sustain fish, than Alar coating the Apples, then global cooling.

The establishment eventually settled on the big daddy of environmental scare theories, the Chicken Little, the henny-penny, the sky is falling hysteria of man-made global warming which, when this term proved to be unpopular and unsustainable, was changed to climate change. There is, indeed, evidence to suggest that the earth atmosphere is warming and that this warming is probably caused by air pollution. There is, however, insufficient scientific evidence at this time to indicate that this phenomena constitutes an impending crisis, one that would require the United States to de-industrialize, especially as the same globalists who are calling for this are effectively giving a green-light to Communist China and other nations to continue to build pollution spewing coal plants. Inventors, with support from government investment and with pro-business regulation, should be able to solve or ameliorate this problem over time and should be able to function in an atmosphere that eschews the histrionics.

Satanic religious cults have always operated in the shadows of western society and culture and much has been written exposing their secrets and their various symbols which often appear in broad daylight as the logos of some of our most prominent institutions of business and culture. While these images and symbols have no more power over us than did the ancient graven images of biblical times, and while the only power and influence that they hold is that which people endow them with, we ought to nevertheless study this issue, and learn to detect these images as a means to glimpse into the possible satanic nature of those who are fully witting of their meaning. Indeed, satanic imagery is saturating our culture today, our movies, art, music, and other forms of popular culture. We would be wise to learn to detect this trend and to then fearlessly call this out at every opportunity.

The occultic satanic beliefs of the ruling elite today might be incapsulated by a brief study of the beliefs of late 19th Century

Russian philosopher and mystic Helena Petrovna Blavatsky, the co-founder of the Theosophical Society. Theosophy, which seeks to unite all of the world religions in correspondence with a one world government, constitutes a synthesis between magic and mysticism and the pseudo-scientific racist theory of evolution as it was posited by naturalist and enlightenment saint Charles Darwin. The Theory of Evolution, putting aside the controversial question of its scientific merit, provides a raison deter for an establishment seeking to change, alter, or evolve human nature. Indeed, evolution provides the justification, wrapped in the garb of science as it is, of the satanic idea of creating a new and more enlightened biological form of humanity.

The Darwinian theory holds that different races of human beings exist in a dynamic condition of collective flux in terms of their approximate and ever moving location on the ladder of evolution. The process of evolution, which is the process of natural selection or, in more plain language, the process of breeding, involves different races, or perhaps this could be described as different sub-species to be more literally Darwinian, are at either more or less superior levels of evolution. This explanation of the Theory of Evolution, while vigorously denied by its adherents, is unavoidable when the theory itself is studied and understood, which holds that a select species evolves to the point of superiority by which a segment of its members will transform into a new and superior species.

This biological idea, which supplanted the God based understanding that every human being, created in the image of God is, as such, equal. The Theory of Evolution would go on to form the scientific and moral underpinning for the Nazi movement which was involved in calibrating and estimating different races due to their alleged levels on the evolutionary chain. Karl Marx, who was hired by the secretive League of the Just to write *The Communist Manifesto* in 1848, grafted Darwin's biological theory into his social theory. Marx incorporated the idea of biological evolution based upon race, which is classic and explicit Darwinism, applying it to an examination of class and class conflict. Thus, for Marx, society would pass through levels of social evolution, from feudalism, to capitalism, to socialism, and finally to the utopian worldwide condition that he called Communism. This would be when mankind would no longer be fettered by such forms of false consciousness as belief in God, the family, property, the right to trade in goods and services, the nation-state, individual consciousness, and any of the other ideas or institutions that might foster inequalities. Under Communism, Marx opined, such institutions would *wither away* and all of humanity would become one gigantic ant colony.

In *The Secret Doctrine*, Blavatsky established the idea of *The Intelligent Evolution of All Existence.* (25.) Blavatsky wrote of a highly evolved spiritual hierarchy of higher and exalted beings who she called *Masters of Ancient Wisdom*. Blavatsky illustrates a race theory that, I would contend, is secretly held, with variations and different terminology, to this very day by the satanic elite. Indeed, it has been reported, Hitler kept a copy of her book on his night table.

Mankind is obviously divided into god-informed men and lower human creatures. The intellectual difference between the Aryan and other civilized nations and such savages as the South Sea Islanders, is inexplicable on any other grounds. No amount of culture, nor generations of training amid civilization, could raise such human specimens as the Bushmen, the Veddhas of Ceylon, and some African Tribes, to the same intellectual level as the Aryans, the Semites, and the Turanians so called. The 'sacred spark' is missing in them and it is they who are the only inferior races on the globe, now happily – owing to the wise adjustment of nature which ever works in that direction – fast dying out. Verily mankind is 'of one blood,' but not of the same essence. We are the hot-house, artificially quickened plants in nature, having in us a spark, which in them is latent. (26.)

Julian Huxley could be viewed as a penultimate specimen of an establishment doyen who embraced and advanced the beliefs and tactics of what I describe as the satanic conspiracy. He played a key role in the thinking and the direction of the post World War II international establishment. Huxley's grandfather, biologist T. H. Huxley, was the primary figure promoting Charles Darwin's book, *On the Origins of Species by means of Natural Selection, or the Preservation of Favored Races in the Struggle for Life*. This book, which scientized racism and served to de-throne the human being as a unique creation in the image of God, hit the international elite like a thunderclap at the time of its 1859 publication. Huxley put this book, which would markedly change and alter how we perceive existence and our role in it, on the map with his review in the London Times. T. H. Huxley, who coined the term *agnostic,* would go on to a career of publicly debating and mocking religious leaders and thinkers.

Zoologist Sir Julian Huxley was the President of the British Eugenics Society, the founding Director of the United Nations Educational, Social and Cultural Organization, UNESCO, a founding member of the World Wildlife Fund and the first President of the British Humanist Association. Huxley is credited as the main author of the post-World War II evolutionary consensus by which eugenics and evolution were given a new and spiffy looking coat of paint after its image had become somewhat murky due to the Nazi Holocaust. Speaking at a 1936 lecture, named for Eugenics founder and Darwin cousin Francis Galton, Huxley noted: *Once the full implications of evolutionary biology are grasped, eugenics will inevitably become part of the religion of the future, or of whatever complex of sentiments may in the future take the place of organized religion.* (27.)

Huxley wrote what could be viewed as the blueprint for what would become the new world religion, a form of amoral atheism that would leave in place the outward trappings and rituals of conventional religion while replacing the philosophy, the theology and moral and ethical code with the Theosophic, occultist, internationalist agenda. Huxley's evolutionary humanism would work in a manner similar to that of the Fabian movement of late 19th Century Britain. The Fabians sought to implement an amoral form of international socialism by means of stealthily changing the meaning of the laws of nations by changing the practical meaning of the words that make up those laws while leaving the words themselves in place. The nation state, in the Fabian scheme, would also remain in place, at least by appearance, but the actual power of governance would be transferred to an international body of unelected elitists, perhaps those to whom Blavatsky might have called the masters of ancient wisdom. The American organization that most closely resembles the Fabian agenda and approach is the American Civil Liberties Union.

UNESCO, which is a branch of the United Nations, has been referred to as the school board of the world. Julian Huxley, its first director, authored *UNESCO: Its Purpose and its Philosophy* where he wrote: *The task before UNESCO...is to help the emergence of a single world culture, with its own philosophy and background of ideas, and with its own broad purposes.* Huxley noted that UNESCO would word toward promoting *the ultimate need for world political unity*, UNESCO would prepare *all peoples with the implications for the transfer of full sovereignty from separate nations to world organization...*UNESCO *can do a great deal to lay the foundations on which world political unity can later be built.* (28.)

UNESCO would sponsor the 1964 *International Symposium on Health, Education, Sex Education and Education for Home and Family Living* in Hamburg, Germany. At that conference, Huxley presented protocols that would become sex education noting that: *It will be one of the major tasks of the philosophy division of UNESCO to stimulate...the quest for a restatement of morality that shall be in harmony with modern knowledge and adapted to the fresh functions imposed by the ethics of the world today.* The conference further noted that *sex education should begin at an early age.* (29.)

The ultimate satanic agenda involves an elite clique of man attempting to control who lives and who dies as, such control, is the ultimate expression of a conspiracy to replace God. This agenda was scientized and legitimized by Charles Darwin's cousin and close collaborator Francis Galton who coined the term Eugenics which is derived from the ancient Greek term for good birth. Eugenicist Julian Huxley expressed the essence of this in a 1947 article called The Uniqueness of Man:

If so, then we must plan our eugenic policy along some such lines as the following...The lowest strata, allegedly less well-endowed genetically, are reproducing relatively too fast. Therefore birth-control methods must be taught them; they must not have too easy access to relief or hospital treatment lest the removal of the last check on natural selection should make it too easy for children to be produced or to survive; long unemployment should be a ground for sterilization, or at least relief should be contingent upon no further children being brought into the world; and so on. That is to say, much of our eugenic program will be curative and remedial merely, instead of preventive and constructive. (30.)

The satanic conspiracy continues marching forward in its long war against God, nature, and the natural rights of the human being under God. I would argue that the satanic conspiracy has achieved the high ground at the present time. They are working at break-neck speed to close the gap in terms of controlling the means of communication through dominance of the technologies of internet communication. They are developing technologies associated with virtual reality, the internet of things, Transhumanism, electronic voting, and massive computer data-bases that collect and categorize information on every citizen by means of spying.

We do not know exactly what the conspirators are doing as the operate in secret and the often operate through their formal, government-sponsored secret societies that we refer to as the intelligence community, the national security apparatus, or what President Donald Trump accurately identified as the Deep State.

My intention here is not to be pessimistic or to be overly alarmist as, besides being a natural optimist, I believe that truths will ultimately prevail, because they are true, and that the forces of freedom will ultimately be stronger than the conspiracy that seeks to suppress God-given freedoms. While I believe that the good and the right will ultimately prevail, my concern is at what cost? Given the record of the satanic conspiracy, holocaust, genocide, democide, starvation, population decimation, totalitarianism, mind control, I would suggest that my concerns in this regard are quite real.

CONCLUSION

Satan is everywhere. Satan is both inside and outside of us. Satan permeates our past, our present and our future. Satan is the force that draws us away from God and, because we are imperfect images of God and we are not God, we often find ourselves caught in the middle of two centrifugal forces. Satan is the anti-God because Satan is false, and God is true. While God is self-evident, Satan is the great deceiver who reels us in with irresistible power and magnetism and who dazzles us with lies that are so slick and are so powerful that we often find them hard to detect. Our purpose in life as individuals, and the hallmark of our character, is to know God and to reject Satan, to know truth and to reject falsehood, to know virtue and to reject vice. Indeed, while we cannot know all things, because we are not God, we can nevertheless know enough about existence and morality, and we can know enough about God to reject Satan both in our own lives and within our societies.

Our lives and our societies are, as such, saturated with Satan, they always have been, and they will be until Almighty God decides otherwise. Every major decision that we make, as individuals and as societies, involves weighing and measuring complex factors that include elements of God and Satan. While God is truth, Satan is also, paradoxically, a form of truth because Satan is an inversion of truth and, as such, an inversion of truth is also true. Yet, I hasten to mention, the satanic principle, given that the essence of that principle is, paradoxically, based upon a lie, is to manufacture half-truths and falsehoods and to market those half-truths and falsehoods as truths. Indeed, individuals and movements that claim to hold the power to abolish Satan, that claim that they can effectuate a perfected utopian world free of evil, as was the case historically with various Gnostic movements and with more modern utopian movements such as Nazism, Communism and Radical Islam, are themselves satanic because they embraced a fundamental falsehood regarding human nature and the embrace of such a falsehood, or a lie, holds within it the most fundamental essence of the satanic principle.

I feel compelled to conclude this brief book, unfortunately, with some grim speculations in terms of where I believe the Satanic Conspiracy now stands in the world. I will do this out of an understanding that by investigating and by exposing these evil practices, and by exposing the evil ideas that support and sanction those practices, the evil will be abated and set on its heels by good God-fearing people and nations. What is required in order to make this happen is a simultaneous clear and unequivocal declaration of that which is good and that tis declaration must be accompanied by a thorough investigation of this evil. I cannot prove that the speculation that I present here is true, which is why I am avoiding naming names, and I hope, and I pray, that I am wrong. While I may, indeed, be wrong, or be partially wrong, nevertheless, the amount of rancor, and the media blackout over even merely speculating on these topics, is itself suspicious in my opinion.

I am referring here to rumors, and in many cases more than rumors but evidence, that various forms of child sex trafficking, pedophilia, torture, ritual murder, human slavery, satanic ritual and other dark practices have reached an international level of critical mass within the highest and the most secretive levels of the ruling international establishment. Rumors abound that these practices involve elements of an international elite that has turned more than ever in the direction of open and unabashed satanism. I believe that increased levels of censorship by the establishment media has caused an effective information blackout of these topics and has, as such, rendered any meaningful and legitimate investigation of criminal activity to be extremely difficult.

I believe that this international and interlocking satanic movement is underscored by and finds scientific legitimacy in by the new science of Transhumanism which should be viewed as an ongoing part of an age-old satanic agenda that seeks to alter human nature which, de-facto, represents an attempt to overthrow God and natural existence. Early 19th Century author and enlightenment figure Mary Shelley blew the whistle on this in her fictional 1818 novel *Frankenstein, or the Modern Prometheus* as, indeed, the ultimate dream of this satanic elite has always been to literally create new human beings, to create life out of non-life, to evolve the human species or race. Rumors of human experimentation, cloning, the implanting of computer chips, satellite control, mind control techniques and other modalities that once might have been in the realm of the horror genre or science fiction are now becoming true.

We must move forward in our drive to identify and expose this evil and we must proceed with courage, with care, with perseverance, and with faith in God, the creator of the Universe and the giver of the Law.

Notes

1. Descartes, Rene: Meditations on First Philosophy, pub. 1641, p. 29.
2. "(The matter of the Creation of) a human being is put together in the womb of the mother in forty days, and then he becomes a clot of thick blood for a similar period, and then a piece of flesh for a similar period. Then Allah sends an angel who is ordered to write four things...then the soul is breathed into him"
Sahih al-Bukhari, 4:54:430
3. Pirkei Avot 1:14, translated Charles Taylor.
4. Babylonian Talmud, Shabbat 31a
5. Matthew 22:35-40
6. Leviticus 19:2
7. Leviticus 23:22
8. Leviticus 19:10
9. Chambers, Whittaker Witness, Regnery 1952
10. Ibid
11. Robison, John: Proofs of a Conspiracy: Against all the Religions and Governments of Europe, carried on in the secret meetings of Freemasons, Illuminati, and Reading Societies, 1797
12. Barruel, Abbe Agustin, Memoirs Illustrating the History of Jacobinism
13. Boston 1775, History, analysis, and unabashed gossip about the start of the American Revolution in Massachusetts
14. Ibid.
15. The President and the Press: Address before the American Newspaper Publishers Association, April 27, 1961, John F. Kennedy Presidential Library and Museum.
16. The Masonic Oath
17. Ibid
18. The President and the Press.
19. Billington, James H., Fire in the Minds of Men: Origins of the Revolutionary Faith. Routledge, 1998
20. Report from Iron Mountain, Wikipedia
21. Wormser, Rene, Foundations: Their Power and Influence
22. Report from Iron Mountain, Ibid
23. NBC News, Former Israeli Security Chief says extraterrestrials exist, and Trump knows about it, Dec. 8, 2020
24. HuffPost, The State of the Nation: A Dictatorship without tears, Jan. 12, 2016
25. Blavatsky, Helena Petrovna, The Secret Doctrine, the Synthesis of Science, Religion and Philosophy, 1888.
26. Ibid. Vol 2, p 421.
27. Hubback, David, Julian Huxley and Eugenics, The Eugenics Society, 1989
28. Huxley, Julian, UNESCO: Its Purpose and its Philosophy, 1947
29. Irvine, Janice M., Talk About Sex: The Battles over Sex Education in the United States, U California Press, 2002
30. Huxley, Julian, Man in the Modern World. Chatto & Windus, London. Originally published in The Uniqueness of Man, 1941, p.66

Index